THE THRONE PERPENDICULAR TO ALL THAT IS
HORIZONTAL

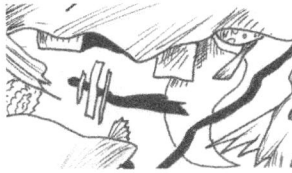

THE THRONE
PERPENDICULAR
TO ALL THAT IS
HORIZONTAL

poems

September 18, 2009 – January 25, 2010

Daniel Abdal-Hayy Moore

The Ecstatic Exchange
2014
Philadelphia

For quotes any longer than those for critical articles and reviews,
contact:
The Ecstatic Exchange,
6470 Morris Park Road, Philadelphia, PA 19151-2403
email: abdalhayy@danielmoorepoetry.com

First Edition
ISBN: 978-0-578-14052-0 (paper)
Published by *The Ecstatic Exchange,*
6470 Morris Park Road, Philadelphia, PA 19151-2403

Also available from *The Ecstatic Exchange:*
Knocking from Inside, poems by Tiel Aisha Ansari

Cover and inside drawings by the author
Author's photo © Lou Wilson

بســـ ﷽

DEDICATION

To
Shaykh ibn al-Habib
(and the continuation of the Habibiyya)
Shaykh Bawa Muhaiyuddeen,
all shuyukh of instruction and ma'arifa
and
Baji Tayyaba Khanum
of the unsounded depths

✻

The earth is not bereft
of Light

CONTENTS

AUTHOR'S INTRODUCTION

We're born into a relationship with theology. Nurtured in the womb by other than our means, born into the world at large, at very large, from our meditative seclusion, our *khalwa*, the Arabic for spiritual retreat (often practiced in a closet-like room just enough for a devotee to sit comfortably) we emerge into a theological world, willy-nilly. As soon as we take a breath of worldly oxygen we're in a tight relationship with the whole God-system, as believers or non-believers, until our last breath leaves us. After which (depending on the tradition we've followed) another relationship begins, fraught with possibilities, from pre-descriptions, that either does or does not entail a defining theology, a judgement, depending (God help us) on our previous strongly held opinions on the matter, and how we've lived our days in accord with them.

Some people see God everywhere from the first. It could be argued that we all begin as saints. Some see gods, and some see no god at all, ever, but it seems to take a lot of effort. There's early delight in everything that comes to us, for the most part, and we respond with what somehow we've been given, happy or sad. This carries through our lives, and that first kernel is nurtured or starved, cultivated or repressed, while the God-seeing ones seem to live one way and the God-negating ones another. The revelation of the Holy Qur'an from Allah begins with a highly positive announcement, and very quickly responds to those who will reject it. Everyone one, pro or con, has some kind of relationship with theology.

Now, the Throne of the title of this collection of poems, refers to the "seatedness" if you will, of God, established "within" His creation metaphorically (God neither within nor without), in kingly fashion. He's not, in Islamic belief, remote, but in a verse, says, "He is closer to you than your jugular vein." But in Muslim/Sufi theology, while metaphors are acceptable ways of picturing the Creator, the more extensive and mystically vast way is that He (oops, there it is again!) has no likeness, no metaphor, nothing is like Him (metaphorically speaking), He is beyond all possible human conceptions, however vast, however even seemingly indifferent to us. Perhaps even the atheists can relate to this. Because then we're left with a material world that goes on like clockwork, all by itself. But the theology is that everything, yes, everything is a *manifestation* of Allah, brought into being by his fiat, *Kun fa yakun* (*Be!* and it is) and nothing living can do without Him, nothing, and the whole creation itself is "meanings set up in images." It's a marvelous tension, and a tension for the Marvelous! For the Marvelous (with a tip of the hat to American poet, Philip Lamantia) is the way things really are, from the Unseen inward and outward. And awe and bewilderment can be said to be our most appropriate stance before it all.

So in the title, it's a Throne that is perpendicular, at an always angle, to all that is in our and all worlds, while still being "seated" (only "as it were") within it, and Allah "seated" upon it. And this is our present and ever-present reality, in all its manifestations. It's a way of seeing and a way of being, and everyone down to the minutest mouse, is in "theological" relation to it.

Oh, that feather floating through the air, and that ant at the water drain! Yes, you there... *you too!*

One of the two Qur'anic passages that mention the name "Loving" associates it with the divine Throne: "He is the Forgiving, the Loving, the Lord of the Throne" (85:14-15) Elsewhere, the Qur'an tells us that it is God as the All-Merciful who is sitting on the Throne. The tradition typically understands the Throne to designate the outermost sphere of the heavens, which encompasses the whole cosmos. It follows that God's mercy embraces everything, as the Qur'an says explicitly (7:156).

— Chittick, *Ibn 'Arabi Heir to the Prophets (page 45)*

HIS PERPENDICULAR THRONE

Love for Allah is a Great Simplicity
while love for all else complexifies redundancy...

Oh face of my single beloved
disappearing around the edges

At the heat center of your graceful animation
is His Light pouring through you

in floods from His perpendicular Throne

5/19/2008 (from *The Fire Eater's Lunchbreak*)

I CAN'T SAY

I can't say
nor can I not say

nor unsay
that which I said

Nor will say
what I can't say

to say
what can't be said

9/18

INSIDE THIS LITTLE HEART OF MINE

Inside this little heart of mine
a universe resides

I don't have to travel far to find
a Samarkand or New Hebrides

The tomes of Alexandria's shelves
the corals of Adriatic deeps

The moons of Jupiter or Mars
or where extinguished starlight sleeps

It's here encoiled in these valves
these chambers with their echoings

across vast cloudlands and near breaths
the same for paupers as for kings

And in particular its Lord
by every ant and flea adored

9/18

I WANT A ROSE

I want a rose so gloriously gorgeous
it sails on its own through all the

windows in the world

and comes up in front of every face
with a look so sunny it puts the

sun to shame

For in that is God's great generosity
to have given us all that which can

sense what is real

And the touch of the petals' edges brings
sanity back to the insane

whose only error is not to
recognize this rose

even when its scent fills our hearts
thinking it conspires against us

For all beauty has a backside and that
backside is its opposite but

behind that is a beauty even more

radiant than its front side

that only some might
glimpse with compassion

Yet to die in the fullness of this rose
riding on a stampede of velvet red horses

across the rocky horizons of the moon or Mars

is to go up the stem into full bloom
to cause another to bend to

inhale its annihilating fragrance

9/19

THE DAUGHTER OF THE OGRE

The daughter of the ogre was actually
quite nice though she tried to explain the

impact he had on everyone by mentioning
his unfortunate childhood

Lucrezia Borgia's husband unbeknownst to
everyone was a splendid chap who often

substituted her caffeine-rich drinks with
camomile tea to soften her venality

The Pharaoh's wife is a well-known saint
who spent many a night on her knees not only

praying for his complete transformation
but for the general good of all mankind

We ourselves are often split down the middle
the two halves bound by the subtlest of chains

almost pure gossamer that barely restrains
the darkness of one half from encroaching entirely

on the radiance of the other
and the tug-of-war is often excruciating

It's just lucky the territory is as
vast as it is and that it even contains

distant galaxies and glorious stars circulating in their
nimbus of heavens like singing children

or else our two sides would suffocate even the
most stalwart among us and we might

go down to the dregs without a fight
rather than that golden part of us keeping its

eye on something majestically intangible outside our
universe entirely that something that has

called itself a Name and a divine Pronoun to
call our better half to His Totality

and our fragmentation to a Unity in which it
turns out what made the ogre's daughter so nice was

that part of the ogre himself who on
late nights by moonlight wept at his

slaughters and repented the fangs of his
fiery breath

9/23

RAIN

The rain is the same everywhere

but the sound depends on the

way the drains are made

9/23

THE TINCTURE

for Salsabeel Syed Sanders

In the shadow was the tincture
in the tincture was the drops

In the drops were worlds within
worlds silently spinning

In the spinning was the singing
in the singing were the words

In the words were the meanings
turning the earth red and the

sky pearl

In the pearl was translucence
in translucence was brilliance

In brilliance was the original light
of the heavens and the earth

In the earth was the heavens
in the heavens were all the stories

In all the stories we reside and
will do so till the end

In the end is that flicker that
indicates transition and in

transition is the latch that
indicates beginning

In the beginning is anticipation of
what is to come

In what is to come is the inevitable outcome
and its consequential ligaments

leading to further beginnings all of which
must end and in their

majestic or degenerate endings
lie all our tragedies and joys

In our joys are fresh starts
that look out through a baby's eyes

at the world as it passes and
casts its animate shadows

and in its shadows are the tinctures
in the tinctures are the drops

In the drops are worlds within
worlds silently spinning

9/24

A LITTLE MOUSE IN A HOLE

A little mouse in a hole in the house
sings to the moon with the

sweetest of squeaks

Crows can only caw but caw they do
as they fly into the sky's maw then

into trees for their morning Conference of the Birds
squawking and cawing for all they're worth

The giraffe it's said also vocalizes but at
decibels so high or so low (I can't recall)

humans can't hear with the naked ear

Stars also sing in perfect
pitch though of strange keys

and peculiar harmonies you'd maybe
have to be in a front row seat among star debris

to correctly hear
and then you might find angels and

space-demons also leaning in to listen

Light and sound and space and the
creatures who dwell therein...

What a thrilling ensemble we all are
singing to our deity in the

best harmony hoping to be heard the way
we've been created to sound

in light and space
while we go through our

paces

9/25

A STAR FELL INTO OUR CUP

for Shaykh Nooruddeen Durkee

A star fell into our cup
and transformed the drink in it

A figure like a comet-tail followed it
and those who saw it tasted it

For a while the star was a light unto itself
but a small group of people gathered around

to taste it

One taste was all it took to get it
though only those who already knew something of its

taste inside got it

Soon it was being ladled out to everyone
and no one who had even a sip of it

would forget it

Of course some tried to drain it or
ban it but that only increased the tangy

taste of it

It was a star-studded ocean that
filled that cup and no one could

drink all of it

But it was distributed
and in its distribution was a miracle

central to it

That even if just a drop of it fell into
another cup of something else

it totally transformed it

Such was its strength that it
transforms even today though it was

centuries ago that what happened to it
happened to it

The cup has even been repeatedly shattered
though its original shape has

always adhered to it

Anyone who wants a drink can taste it
but no one can walk away from it

A shimmer precedes it
and a stillness after just one sip of it

follows it

9/26

TO SLIDE DOWN THE CASCADE

"If you want to slide down the cascade"
they were fond of saying

"you'll have to get a ladder to the stars
to get the right advantage" that's

how dwarfed everything else is
to its giant perspective

And if you want to plumb the ocean's
deeps you'll have to be a

sea anemone making little flexible
squirts downward though you

may not reach the deepest crevice or
crevasse to find pure blackness and

the occasional phosphorescent critter
with its little lamp on a stalk before its

eyes as it navigates not blind but
somewhat disadvantaged yet perfectly

adapted and thrilled to be puffing along
here miles underwater

And if we want to be a human being and not
a sleepwalker head in clouds and

feet in Hell I guess we'll have to
get busy to get the right vantage point and

the proper navigational headlight in our
various deeps airy if not watery

And in the great cobbler's laboratory where we're
fitted with true traveling shoes for our

strange and punctual lifespan
we might get acquainted with the

staff and particularly the Head of Staff
to insure a proper fit and some

sweet acceleration with enough
pauses to really enjoy the vistas opening

out above and around us both its
heights and depths and tall cascades

and the sacrificial dues owed
for our ample ramblings

9/29

THE SPHINX'S NOSE

The sphinx's nose is crying out for
compensation and restitution

to be placed squarely back on that
weather-beaten face in Giza to be made less

flat by a proboscal protuberance
but of course it's mostly dust by now

and not sitting under a sheet in some
thief's garage or museum basement waiting for

facial reconciliation

The Wingéd Victory would like her
head back and the Venus de Milo her arms

and millions of penises would like to be
reattached to their statuesque owners

knocked off through the ages by
prudes or rascal vandals

Glaciers would like to be restored
and many polar bears are considering

running for the Senate to pass a
bill or two if that would help

I'm not sure I want to be twenty-five again
after all with the same arc ahead of me

I had then to now but a little more
robustness and a few new memory chips

wouldn't be bad

Yet time has its ravages as it
cuts its way to the original sea of

both its goal and its origin
slicing and dicing canyons and

roadways through matter and events
and when time melts away will there be

all these things now cut off left in
mounds of debris or will

there only be timelessness at last?

Which seems to have been the intended
goal all along

for stone noses whole heads arms and
even penises in this world as we

willingly or reluctantly intact or
lopped

clock in to the next

9/30

EXPATRIATES

The expatriates who were left behind
got together saying there was

strength in numbers but they
never got the handshake

They tried settling in the little
habitable pockets that still

experienced a semblance at least
of the seasons and the ability to grow things

pitching strange tents in crevasses and
singing bits of old songs they

remembered for morale

But it wasn't the same
and they couldn't kid themselves

too much longer what with the wild beasts

wandering freely now in even the
urban ruins and the way the

rain slanted and the snow had a
pink tinge and they

couldn't get mirrors or even
smooth water or glass surfaces

to reflect their images back to them
however much they tried sneaking into the

frame suddenly yet still finding an empty space where
a face should be

Candles went on spontaneously
and motors died and were

unrevivable

We tried to call them to
give them hope but the

lines were always busy even though
they never used them

and there was that continual
grinding noise as if the earth on its

axis needed some grease to revolve
smoothly

among the still-twinkling stars
where God's Voice can be heard

echoing as He
moves in His private chambers

10/2

EVERYONE'S STORY

Everyone's story turns out to be
different than you thought

The sweet old couple who love horses
turn out to be terrorists

The ticket taker on the train turns out to be
a retired lion tamer

The blond young man with the bad leg
is an Olympic swimmer

The coil inside us all unrolls in unforeseen
unfurlings

presenting a face outward that may hide the
inward countenance whose expressions are

storytellers of the most outlandish possibilities

The Mongolian explorer who looks like a
retired German stamp collector

The happy pair who shoot each other
around the next corner for seemingly

no reason
though the details of their histories coincide in

murderous combat

and the other pair at the outdoor café who
spend three hours in complete silence

turn out to be in such harmony no words at all
are needed

A time comes when a divine floodlight
illuminates every face in perfect resolution

to show to us and to everyone else
the leather-bound sagas that got us here

and through it all our utter dependence on
The One Actor in all of it Who both

inspires us and
supports us on the road

10/4

INNER EAR

Merchants carry within their ships
merchandise

Death carries within its skirts
decrees

Seasons change from winter to winter
and back again

Death is the change that doesn't change
at all

Water flows through rock canyons
cutting them

Death is the slice of sweet relief
releasing us

Fear of heights can cause some
to fall

Fear of death can cause some
to rise

The edge of one moment leads by an angle
to the next

Death is a painful squeeze that

transforms us utterly

In a room without windows we
can't see the other side

In life we learn death is a
stern enigma

A door is opened that floods the room
with light

Death tears down walls and leaves
everyone illumined

Someone can come and take us away
any moment

Death comes once and takes us
in its embrace

I hear the music of silence in my
inner ear

The breath of death is the stopping of breath
that is all breath

No one truly knows of death
but God

Oh gently take us to You
when You take us

10/5

A PERSON IN PRAYER

A person in prayer
is a huge boulder in a giant valley

that's been curled into itself for
millennia but now emits a

gentle hum wild flowers and
valley grasses turn to

and wild goats scratch their
itchy skins against

A person in prayer
is a sudden silence in a busy street

trucks street-machinery taxis train-horns
people in crowds passing

construction sites
all at once become mute

so mute you can hear the moist

emergence of a moth from its cocoon
and the shifting of clouds

Hamlet couldn't kill Claudius at prayer
fearing his soul was heaving heavenward

Physical changes on earth take place
when a person is at prayer

Ask any redwood mountain crest or canyon glacially
exposed to the sky whose river at its

base reflects both sun and stars

A clod of earth suddenly ashimmer

A sound like a galactic flute
linking distances

A murmur more articulate than a
Prime Minister's address to the nation

Showers of its intonations rising above
earth's magnetic core like

hair streaming out as it speeds through space

on its way to the sacred zero where
all prayer goes

10/6

ZERO

Multiply your self by zero
— Baji Tayyeba Khanum

*Fa yafnaa, thumma yafnaa, thumma yafnaa, fa
kaana fanaauhu 'ayna 'l-baqaa'* ("He was effaced,
then effaced, then effaced, until effacement
became his very subsistence" — Sufi saying)

With a sense of bird-like elation
he began to introduce zeros into every conversation

so that he might begin speaking by
clearly enunciating a large round zero

and then adumbrate whatever might need to
follow in grammatical detail and

end it all with a zero or two for
final emphasis with the net effect of

erasing all that went before

His sentences grew shorter and his
zeros more numerous

Adjectives almost entirely disappeared
and what was left were the

odd detritus sticking up out of the
sand of verbs and nouns doing whatever

was needed to be done though within their
hardy fabric you could find a few

zeros expanding and nudging even the
activity of concision and action aside

The zeros beamed zoomed radiated and
drew everything into their vacuum

Edges difficult to endure during the day
were softened and even effaced by a

certain cunning placement either
before or after or both of a set or

two of zeros

How he could be so rhapsodic with these
emptinesses and emptyings was almost

unfathomable for he really took great
delight in launching them like weather balloons into

the skies of normal communication until
those skies silvered and then misted over and

became drained of color as they slipped almost
surreptitiously into a row of awaiting zeros

Soon he himself grew simpler and more profound
more still in his being as well as more

laconic in his presence

The world around him became less like a
world around him and more like a

world of silhouettes and puffs of smoke
rays of sudden light and very

definite darkness
but ultimately circling around and

around in a melodious circulation with the
circumference of a giant zero as

great as an ocean or the very sky itself
and the only thing remaining was in fact

the Radiant Beauty of the One only non-zero
the only Zero-Resistant

before Whom everything else in creation is zero

Who introduced us all to zero in His
infinite compassion for the very

breaths we breathe and deaths we must
survive as we

head out through ultimate zero to

One

10/7

HARD THUD

Hard thud at the back of the stairs

Slap of a skiff against a pier

Tin cans falling off a fence

A chained dog howling all night

Late laboratories of people hunched over screens

Grasses growing silently in fields

Slip of clouds across and through each other

Early morning kitchen filled with sunlight

Mathematical formula writing itself out in the
mathematician's mind around midnight

Developments in a mineshaft deep in the earth

A glass vase falling to pieces in an undisturbed tomb

Actor's entrance stage right who
strides to the center of the stage and

sings his lines

Nurse fainting from fatigue and a
young doctor coming on duty in fresh scrubs

Squeal of brakes around a mountain curve

Fresh and fragile rain falling on alpine housetops

Sheep huddling together at an angle on a hill

Landslide that covers a village in ten minutes

Gradual blackout of a solar eclipse

Things going on in another galaxy

A child playing in a sandbox all by herself

First smile on the face of a newborn

10/10

JOHN KEATS

Death threw open the long door to John Keats
early enough for him to write a

handful of immortal poems
which he dutifully did

Though not a ballroom dancer he got the
Dance of Death down step by step on the

foolscap floor he knew best as the
dark forest closed around him

A white moth by candlelight looks
bigger than it is

but if the shadow it cast frightened
John to greatness we can be grateful

each flutter looked fatter

He was scrambling up a landslide
as fast as it slid

but coming from an ocean he entered an
ocean in the end

and disappeared
written on its water

10/13

BEFORE I GO

Before I go I'd like to recommend
the mile high door that

opens from the inside
the ocean voyage that

circulates around in our blood
and a visit and salutation to

all and every bird however plain or
tatty you can find for their

pleasure is flight and their
loyalty is the window they'd

like to fly through into eternity and
not stop until they get there

The days are both short and long
the seasons both come and go

The treasures of the eyes are nothing compared
to the treasures of the heart though

far less tangible or perhaps far more

since that which dazzles darkens
while that which glows warms

And an outreached hand to catch another
is the rope that climbs us out of this

abyss into the bright fields of heaven

Before I go there are so many things I'd
like to recommend other than the

Grand Canyon itself which lies under the
sky a living metaphor of the

deathlessness of death and the utter
dryness of lush abundance

even as its tiny river seen below from

the topmost perspective cuts its
way to the soul

There's rain and its patter on any roof
there's walking among trees and overgrown paths

There's beloved faces coming toward us with their
cheeks and eyelashes and expressions no

words anywhere can adequately capture

I'd recommend the roar of lions and
stampedes of zebra if I could

the nose dive of whales and the
flight straight up of larks before they

loop to descend

I'd recommend the endlessness that
foregoes the ending to this poem

so that recommendation continues
flowing long after it's done

long after I'm done
and my recommendations simply

ring by themselves among the large and
small bells of everything hung

everywhere for our delight
and the wisdom that comes from

hearing them more clearly each time they ring
blossoms into a sky made

golden by that silvery sound

10/15

IF LIGHT WENT BACK

If light went back to what it
was before it assumed so many shapes

we might live in a blinding arctic of light
a complete whiteout of light

but Mercy has fashioned everything in
such perfect balance illumination

stretches across things like silken nylon
and out from the centers of things like

the fanning of giant peacock tails
with our own subsequent miraculous

embubbling of original brightness in a
thought-pause's moment in which

more of the heavens open up to us than are
closed shut and starlight in sweet

drizzles penetrates us with sieve-like
harmoniousness

"Let light in" they say and
"let light out"

And it roams and it blasts but mostly

ebbs and flows in its own

ocean that knows no configuring shores but
darkness

10/18

TWO FRAGMENTS

1 *(from a dream)*

"Then there's the classic option:

Who are we

or who are we *through!*"

10/20

2

With time we're either
heading into or going out of...

whereas in fact we're
afloat in His sea

10/22

THIS EXACT THING

It's this exact thing we are doing
right now that is our life

Pantlegs ballooning shrill above Manhattan
or sitting in an easy chair facing a woodsy window

standing in a shadowy forest following a sound
or in between two gestures that

communicate love to a lover
or the first and foremost beloved of

our lives whom we're convincing right now
this is true

Nothing different is taking place
throughout the energies of our bodies

and the phantom gossamers of our
hearts inclining this way or that

It's almost that we're plants
rooted in the ground

and that it's the ground that's
moving under us taking us to

Shanghai or Madagascar on a

beach idling in the sun or under

Parisian subway girders at night at the
Stalingrad Station needing a

pissoir

And the doom-clock could stop
right in front of us at any moment

while we're imagining flight from this
moment on a horse as

high as the Empire State Building
rearing on its hind legs and

whinnying as it takes off with us
to more benign climes elsewhere

in which our identities may slip from us
as easily as we think they've slipped on

like slippers after a bath

A throne room greater by far than the
size of the known and unknown

universe suddenly resonates with its absolute
stillness

and the voice that is heard there
is the only voice there is

rattling doors and squeegeeing
windows in every direction

as we are right now on the gravel
road where we cast our peculiar shadow

on our way both from somewhere and to
somewhere but at each moment in the

bell tower of our truth pealing with
original iron and original clarity of sound

for all it's worth

10/28

TWO BY THREE

The paddle that breaks the surface of water
propels a canoe

The stroke that strikes a bell in a bell tower
tells time

The crack that occurs at a crack of dawn
ushers in daylight

10/29

OBSCURITIES OF A MOMENT

The obscurities of a moment give way to
the paradoxes of a lifetime

though that shouldn't keep us from trying

And the heights we may climb give way to
quick and steep drops

and yet we climb on shielding our
watery eyes from the glare and

closing our ears to the blare of
car horns

The extent we still have to cross has a
way of lengthening out all over again so that

having got here has a stunted look compared with
where we still have to go

Yet someone's almost always at our side
with a glass of water or a tuna sandwich

and the bell sound faint in the distance
may be the finish line or a school bell

calling us back to those snug desks with
ink well hole and acrid smell of cracked varnish

We can't go on long though before
the sky wants to wrap itself around us

like a lover

and the stars feel like they're studded in our
hair or dazzling in our eyes

And if we have a flushed look it may not be
the Keats disease with countable

days at the end even if in
double digits

but both the urgency and the agency
that will get us there in good time

though *"there"* be a moot point after all
and *"get us"* even somewhat dubious

If we were Inuit and this not the
season of thaw we might drift on an

iceberg under such a sweet pellucid blue sky
even turquoises become shy and have to

lower their eyes

But this is the time of assassins and burglars
and even the best of us might not be

always truth-tellers

We have to throw the latest headlines away
to either side of us as we go

like the wake at each side of the
prow of a speedboat at full throttle

for as Ibn Arabi has said somewhere
"if you set out you will arrive"

and that
should suffice us

10/31

THE SHARP NAIL-SPLITTER

The sharp nail-splitter Who
slices down clean

throws boats into trees
brings two lovers together who've

been tortured
and restores life to a

child's crushed hand

brings a runaway train to a halt
with no passengers injured

and throws a train off a trestle
carrying school children to camp

into a raging abyss below

How are we to be with the one
or the other Who are both

the same?

The house burnt to the ground
with everyone in it

The grandfather who takes his
secret to the grave and the

unsolved murder continues unsolved
as his face grows whiskers then

dissolves around his skull's stiff grin

It's a summer day say
on a pond in a boat with an

umbrella and the two betrothed
calmly boating and he

recites a spontaneous verse to her
and she responds in kind

and the moment is as if lifted
onto the surface of a geyser in

slow motion so smooth and sweet
with the only sound that of

paddles sloshing through water
and the only shadow that of

his form leaning forward to kiss her

11/1

A FLOCK OF STARLINGS

"A flock of starlings" is a
good way to start a poem rather than

"The fire hydrant exploded"

"The goat landed on his four feet" is
better than *"The house was*

sliced off its foundation and
toppled into the sea"

"Grandpa's moustache flowed down
past his mouth" rather than

"Grandpa left the house never to return"

yet at any point in the
twists and turns of a poem we might

encounter rough weather or a fire-flashing
beast guarding the

mouth of a cave

or a stock market crash even if we
began peacefully enough with the

garden growing inch by inch upward
pushing up little green heads and

flowery pastels

Earthquakes might hit in the middle of
a lovely description or

interrupt an exclamation of love

A boat might capsize just as the
reunion's about to take place between

father and son for the
first time in twenty years

Moonlight covers even the roughest
landscape with its silvery pencils

but daylight exposes the ragged
edges and broken stalks

Our eyes tell a story that
changes with the slanting light

whether it comes through the
open window or from the

shining star of the heart

So the starlings might start us
out turning and reappearing in the sky

and the goat simply keep walking

as if nothing happened

and grandpa lick his moustache
while he recounts all this

and across the world the same thing
take place rather than

portions of apocalypse

and when we stand up to leave
the whole world in whatever state

leaves with us

and when we lie down at last
the whole world

lies down

11/2

TO BEGIN AN IMPOSSIBLE PROJECT

To begin an impossible project
lighting lamps across the ocean

laying out mirrors on sand to reflect
the passing of stars

compile all the interlinking stories of the
world from Borneo longhouse to

Manhattan penthouse whose inhabitants
knowingly or unknowingly relate truths in

exotic and quixotic disguises but behind
whose masks and sparkly trinkets

God's identical creatures cavort and
dance to His subtlest tunes to the

end

To build a chain or bridge or
entrance staircase into a dark hall or

giant mythic doorway that opens onto
nothing but reality shorn of illusion

as radiant as grace and fresh as a
newly discovered galaxy that for millennia

hid behind exploding configurations of
stars

To get down in and burrow toward gnostic Light
bringing a few blind creatures along

and finding new linguistic registers to
so irradiate the air that a blaze of white

nearly dissolves all detail and then
evaporates around the one Face that

continually faces us whether we
notice it or not

A building project as well as a project of
demolition angel wing by

angel wing until nothing is left but
flight

11/5

IT'S A SWEET AND HEALING THING

It's a sweet and healing thing now and
then to imagine troops of

angels

Oceans of their luminous beings for
example streaming across the sky

hidden among rocks of Himalayan heights
ready to appear to stranded

climbers either for reasons of
emergency aid or a warm

final embrace

They seem to topple off cliffs of
light among clouds and stretch in

light streams everywhere

Look! There they are over Tokyo!

Swirling with snowflakes around the
onion domes of Moscow!

What did I tell you! You feel
better already!

Pewter in color or the consistency of
quicksilver pulled through the air

Invisible then visible then you turn your
head just a tiny degree and they're

invisible again

Oh no! There's a few scattered among
autumn's last leaves before they

make their final twisting golden descent to the
forest floor

Like gleams of light in spouts of
silver teapots or like

twisting silvery steam at lid-sides of
tea kettles in diagonal sunlight

they twinkle in forward
free fall between planets and

stars to the slow astonishment of
NASA astronomers who keep their

squinted sightings to themselves for
professional reasons

Tumbling and rolling in all
kinds of somersault aerial

motions among flocks of
starlings over morning wheat fields when

dew glistens bedazzle the
tassel tops

Soundless as bicycles but with
just enough squeak in their wings to be

overwhelming

they ribbon through everything
on their way from nowhere to

nowhere and take us completely by
surprise wherever we happen to be

and through whose vast luminous
tunnel of song in circular

rotation we happen to be moving

Eye shine and voice tremor
heartbeat and pulse flutter

There they are

who shall be nameless in their multitudes and
unsung

who each one named in their multitudes

sing their own

song

11/7

THE PARADISE TREE

The brie and burgundy brunch you
want to throw out and the

out-of-the-way bridges in
out-of-the-way towns

Piles of embossed hotel stationary you'll
never use for locational embarrassment

and the shady nature of your journeying
in the first place

all these things to throw out from your
satchel of lifetime collections

appropriated in a tourist mood
after having passed through life's broken

turnstile and gotten your passport stamped
by a bored official two notches away from

deep sleep

We were created to walk semi-nude in a
garden picking fruits and vegetables for our

food and avoiding the strange looking
tree with otherworldly sound track seeming to

come out its trunk
and that no birds roost on

and that laughs to itself in a very
sinister way whose heart obviously

is not on humanity's side

and were created with internal libraries of
particularized esoterica of a

healing nature
absolute encyclopedias of salubrious consciousness

indexed and cross-indexed within us
and at our sensorial fingertips even as the

strange tree we're meant to avoid
gets its own weather around it and is

often shrouded with thick purple mist
and a kind of brimstone hailstorm…

Ah! throw it all out but the
sound of choirs to which you may

add your own voice to its generous
waterfall

crashing through heaven!

11/11

ANOTHER DAY ROLLS UP

Another day rolls up like thunder
over the curve of the earth

Already somewhere the sky is sulfur yellow then
a bronze entrée into sunlight

bringing with it the zillion miniature
cars filled with normal-faced clowns

each with their delicate operas of
longing attainment loss and melodramatic

openings for arias
as animals and insects everywhere

also open their day eyes hungry or in the
case of insects simply continue

doing what they
do so well in the dark

A voice bathes the planet in its deep tones and
high inflections calling some to duty and

releasing others
calling some to romance and some to

their first serious

confrontation with mortality

The gazillion caterpillar roadshow wriggles up over
the earth's curve with a giant heave-ho

sunward to
usher in the day

11/12

WRITE MYSELF INTO OBLIVION

Write myself into oblivion
with all the tics and whiskers

like a giant barrel going over Niagara
with nothing inside it

If a match is lit in a dark room
some light is shed

If a horse finds just one piece of hay
he might be satisfied

The aurora borealis overhead
far outstrips the most intricate

domed interior

If streets are crowded with donkeys
that doesn't mean we have to bray

Something thrilling about all those wheels in a
bicycle race going round and round

Keep the Big Dipper always on your left
and you'll be guided home

Polar bears don't lose themselves in
all that whiteness

Am I gone yet?
I mean really gone?

God replace me with Yourself
selflessly abounded

The shepherd never abandons his
flock at night that the

wolf doesn't take notice

Whatever happened to running boards on cars
that the Keystone Cops could stand on

rounding corners in hot pursuit?

Does sap ever run up a tree
or only down?

The Harrowing of Hell takes place
every couple of days

but people keep popping into it again

If we carry enough heaven around inside us
don't you think it would

lighten the atmosphere?

I mean with all its galaxies and stars
to say nothing of the

angelic hierarchies

Now that's saying a mouthful
and I don't even have a mouth vast enough to

say it with

but we can say it with our hearts
and their magnificent capaciousness

for pulling themselves out of rubble
with a smiling face

Did you hear that rumble?
It's the end of this poem

coming down the road
toward me

11/13

IN MY USUAL DULL TURBIDITY

In my usual dull turbidity
what distant-most star could

descend straight into it to
transform it to streams of sparkling

silver cascading upward against
diamond crags and amethyst hand-and-toe holds

to climb out to
simple sunlight?

The roar of a thousand trains fills the
canyon below and the multiplied

echoes of smoke and locomotives
crisscross space and

efface its majesty
except in the atomic radiance of

God's imploded moment
leaving not traces but the

next breath necessary for life
that buckle thrown around the

belly of the world that

lake on the moon sinking below the

permafrost that heavenly distance between
what we are and what we

will be when we become
ourselves again

11/14

I THROW MY BOOK DOWN

I throw my book down as I write in it
and I throw my pen down after it

and it sails down and down and I
want to throw myself after it

It sails down past redwoods and pines
palms and elms

oceans and shores and coral reefs and
shallows and deeps

I lean over the edge and throw it down
even as I write in it

Slips out of my hands as I hold the
pen that writes in it

and the pen slips out after it

As I write it sails out and sails down
As I speak it inside it coils in a

whirlwind slaking off its skins
thinner and thinner as the pages skim

It sails down and down
and all I might say or sing is

drowned as it sails down
and all that's written in it

pounded down
into powder

and nothing's left but
solid ground

as my book sails down

11/15

THE ROOSTER'S SILENT

The rooster's silent but the dawn
inches up into the dark ever so

slowly as great things take place
on a mountaintop in Siam or

God's Beneficence glows around a
housewife in South Dakota

or natural downflow uncovers a
treasure in the shape of a

lost book that had been
hidden by the Hittites in the rocks

A dazzle leaps out of cracks in the
ground and knocks two shepherd boys

backwards
They've never felt such astonishment before

as their sheep wander among the
dewy grass blades with the

moon still visible
as a scattering of parrots

rainbows through trees

into a blue sky in Brazil

and in overcrowded cities
people start waking up by themselves

each one with a giant compass and a
dissolving mirror in their

hearts they use to navigate by in their
sleep but in

daylight think they should
do so by their own

wits alone

and the housewife in South Dakota
floats down through the shimmering

concentric circles of her tears

and the two shepherd boys run after their
sheep chattering like crazy

and the ancient book waits
patiently for anyone to come along

someday to discover it

11/18

THE STATIONS OF MAJESTY

The stations of Majesty
rise like sculpted mansions of sugar

like dazzling mausoleums of salt
on a plain as wide as the

palms of our hands laid flat
across oceans of turbulence and torpor

where dragons doze and leviathans sleep
until silence comes and awakens them

Then the searchlight of the All-Compassionate Eye
scans the twelve horizons and the

six billion skies for streaks of
calligraphy that spell out the

Majestic Names of He Who is neither
here nor there nor not here nor

not there and this we both

know and don't know by the whole hearts we've been
given as an entrance-pass through

this life to the next by living in
these mansions of sugar and

dazzling mausoleums of salt with eyes wide
open or shut and palms flat or held up in

halt position to flag down whatever
cloud of light might engulf us to

take us away longer than any
forever can be conceived of and

shorter than any breath
and shorter by far

than
any death

11/21

HEART FIRST

It sounds like the ocean's
right at our door

disguised as the air

And space is a four-square
cube that is elsewhere

Presence a felt silhouette of
my self laid up against me

and time a wee little train
going round a track

that never comes back

How do I feel about this
out here on a moon landscape?

Craters for companions
and a few drops of water?

Light tastes as acrid as metal
as it streaks everywhere

We neither greet it nor
wave it goodbye

It just is —
heart first

11/22

HIDDEN IN THE HIDDEN

I know You're here
hidden in the hidden

A Golden Gate sunset
can't hide Your splendor

Behind and through everything
putting two and two together

Your Presence now and then
names itself in traces

Or as I like to call them:
clues left behind in daylight

on everything touched by
He Who created them

happening simultaneously and in
abundant profusion

Post-its™ reminding us
Who's been here before us

as we stand on the
empty bridge in nothing

reading Your signs

As the Manifest One
You're hardest to see

in this pre-silence pre-dawn
where You've sent me

such radiant electricity
all I can do

is praise Thee

11/24

NOT AT ALL?

A soothing word or a
word that scorches

A soft hand caress or a
slap that stings

An embrace that enthralls or
the squeeze of death

Which will it be
desired or decreed?

The round earth's curve rolls
under the sun

Black night flashed with
starlight that surrounds us

The grave is always only
an inch away

The bells of the brightness we
yearn for can always be rung

Cold air surrounds our
hearts in their wintry ovens

Our bodies bring to light our
soul's movements within us

Love is a letter burning
in a high wind

The writing on it first
for us then for everyone

We read it out loud in
every word we speak

Sometimes wind fans it
into a conflagration

Each of its ashes in it
has its own Phoenix

This world's heartbeats continue
their finite mathematics

The next world's unlimited tom-tom
is always calling us

Our response is this one and
that one and the next five million

God grants us everything but
we have to listen harder

Are we a standing mirror to
His light on a tough boulder?

Does His rain fall on nothing at all
or on a slate roof?

Are those inside in conversation
or silent as stone?

Does this poem end on a high note
or not at all?

11/25

POSITIVITY'S PARTY

To persuade the Negative to maintain its
retreat the Positive put on a little

party and invited some guests such as
Socrates the Buddha and some of the more

notable Bodhisattvas and saints

The sun came up and shone and
the seas churned and its waves

beat forward and retreated beat
forward and retreated

Clouds of gray and shafts of light
fell across nations and time

But the Negative kept returning to cause its
array of troubles for both

humankind and the climate

So Positivity tried scare tactics and showed
Negativity the consequences of its

actions by putting on plays such as
Shakespeare's *King Lear* and the

Oedipus Cycle of Euripides and it
did give negativity a start

It hunkered down for a while with a
hanky to its disastrous eyes until

tears were running in long black
streaks down its cheeks

But it would always pluck up its
courage again and return to our

shores to plague even the most
cheerful among us into thinking that

all was futile and the
worst was yet to come

So Positivity resorted to its final but not
ultimate showdown by projecting in as

many ways as possible and on as
many screens among the Manifest as

possible the ineffable glory of Divine
Radiance in everything that

exists from flying gnat to grand
celestial star-birth and cosmic

explosion of rainbow effulgences
and for a brief moment Negativity was

impressed to the point of being
silenced while it took in the sheer

awesomeness around and even
within it

But like a pool of mercury Negativity slid
back into all available spaces and every

even most inaccessible-seeming nook until
it seemed the unending battle would

indeed never end
but Positivity always had some

angle up its armless sleeve to
display in all grandeur

and when enough splendidness
stilled Negativity long enough

everyone could see their way toward
facing the single simple ocean of

rhythmic inevitability with a certain
calm and even somehow a

certain earnest equanimity with the
good Lord's help

the Good Lord King and Owner of all
positivity and negativity and Who

never bestows too much darkness without
sending enough splinters and sparks of

light to illuminate our seesaw
corner of the cosmos at last

amen

11/28
(the 'Eid al-Kabir)

BRIGHT YELLOW MOON

The great belligerent beings
brought nothing with them for their

overnight stay

Nothing could dislodge them from their
impermanent lodgings

You could say their impermanence
went with them wherever they went

like a comfortable dome with
all the amenities

A white tiger might follow them
or a roaring lion

And a howling wolf pack at night
was their kind of music

Little said little asked
everything answered

Their unveiled eyes saw everything unveiled
and said more than their

mouths did

"Stay for the night?"
"Why thank you I'm

just passing through"

The least concern among them might be
our major obsession

which is why what drove us crazy
was only a fly in the room

to them

The same to be said for the world stage
as for our psychological domain

The old mind/body dichotomy was more than
irrelevant to them

it simply didn't exist

Neither where they ended and
we began as well as the

room around us and outside the
windows and down in the

canyons and high in the air with the
condors in their majestic flight and the

whooping cranes in their migrational patterns
home

Secretive about their place of origin
only our common origin was

discussed

and even that only like making shadow
figures on a wall with our hands

for to them we were as impermanent as
they were and only the

light of our absence mattered

the Eternal Presence without us all
was the mast of their ship

passing in the night

and the moon on the horizon
the bright yellow moon

Everything I've left out
best describes them

and the yellow moonlight
on the horizon

the bright yellow moon

11/30

MY LAST POEM

1

Let me not recite you nor
write you down

May you be suffused with
love's radiance enough to

blot out all else

Let you be both a simple
summing up and a forgetting of

all but the most essential though
some glittering of this world's things

might flitter through
just enough to be both a

gallant farewell and an
earthly salutation with

all gratitude for its daily hospitality
though now it might be more

echo than substance more
reverberation with its ghostly glow

than usual

Sitting here age sixty-nine I can't
imagine you and somehow also

I don't want to but from here at
an unknown distance I

address you with a few
goose bumps for you already

exist in perfect and unflinching
form with neither a word more nor

less essential to you
a pure finality without

further editorial correction by
me at least

Will you be like a silver fence
penning earth in against heaven's sheep?

Will some of the next world's music
filter in through its vowels and

syncopated consonants and with
what you will be most populated?

Always looking forward with a kind of
majestic positivity but also a

certain wry humor called for perhaps by
the very fact of your lastness

Angels with quizzical faces or
bewildered cats that will

no longer get their ears scratched?
And restive horses

eager to bound across and be
done with this fly-twitching world

at last?

But enough for now
last poem

Wait for me

2

What am I talking about?
You won't necessarily

know you're last unless you're a
deathbed poem dictated say with

significant pauses between words between
stanzas maybe even between

letters

But you also might have
lastness thrust upon you when you

least expect it
going on and on on your merry way

looking all around as you usually do
right and left and up and down

but not at all thinking to yourself
"This is it! Nothing more to come!"

with all the attendant Whitmanesque
anxiety to get it all in there as a

grand finale even sunlight along a
spiderweb and love letters left in a

broken drawer in the dark

No! You go on and on thinking you're
a poem somewhere in midstream as

usual with the usual hopes for more to come
and the usual thought that this present

poem at flow under the pen could be

the last one at last with
no more ever to follow

But I could be as easily struck down in mid-poem
on a train or at my bedside lap-table and

a final unfinished utterance left as is
forever

So dear last poem whenever and
whomever

be in God's secret plenitude

and I will continue to
empty my self

in order to
be in His

12/1

GROWING UP

Growing up a tree or a toad can't be
all that different from growing up a

soybean or koala bear munching eucalyptus
leaves or a drop of rain or a

flame though they're even more
evanescent than we are growing

up as we do in backyards and vacant
lots the way smallish planetoids must

feel there in space somewhat off to the
side of the great implosions

Growing up through the sacred stages of our
lives the way dragonflies dart across

secret lagoons not so secret to them but
reflective of their image darting across

And though ostensibly all grown up at
this age or that we still

like tops of redwood trees brushing very close to
God's door grow closer and closer ourselves if

we continue moment after moment
to grow to what is essential and not

simply lying in our clutter or continuing to
take copious notes about ourselves those

very selves we'll grow out of in a
flash when the time comes and we might

do well to make more transparent and
flexibly growing under our own

glances and wise commentary now rather than
from afar when there's no more growth

left for us to
grow

12/2

SPECK

I don't know why it is but I love
starting out somewhere in space as a

speck

and then either it expands or the
camera closes in and in until we start to

see mountain ranges and valleys deeper than
the eye can fathom their bases shrouded in

absolute black and there are hovering
purplish mists with blue centers and

yellowish edges as we move down in
closer and closer and our

ears also get accustomed to faint and then
higher register rhythmic sounds as if

space itself were rubbing against itself in a
kind of cicada syncopation

And when some of the mists draw
apart a little we see something like a

peach-colored sunlight or radiance at
least for the sun

(or whatever energizing orb seems central to wherever we
happen to be whether

sun or aureole of atomic juices or
blast that continually renews itself and

sings to itself as it does so)

the sun is nowhere in sight
though now the mists are

surrounding us or perhaps we're
descending through them slowly more and

more and mountain peaks are becoming visible and
radiant geometrical shapes are seen on them

as if mosaics of intricate star shapes or
shapes we associate with the abstracted

graphic representations of stars
and the lines extend it seems infinitely out past

our fields of vision and as we sink
more and more through the mists we

now hear something we associate with flowing
water or giant crashes of surf and

start to see a glittering as if reflected
back to us of large water-like

masses lying between the sheer

mountains whose crags now are
visible and iridescence with scintillating

rainbow colors in bright shimmers runs
vertically and masses now also of something like

vegetation or what we associate with
vegetation or that may be clustered lumps of

something less substantial than vegetation appear
when suddenly we're in circles of

yellow streaks revolving around us
and the voices we've been hearing become

more articulate repeating over and over
syllables both foreign to our ears and

extremely familiar to our hearts

And we begin to see creatures of some kind
as if leaping about on giant swards or

valleys opening out onto polished
greenish esplanades and we see

flashes of crashing watery silvery substance
and over and over the now thick and deep

layering of voices arises until the
sound itself becomes visual or what we

see is actually just the repeated word or
words which themselves project to us

what it is we see and what we
see is so transparent that

everything is as if hanging in sheets of
an enthralling transparency through which we

begin to make out almost the
contours of a face or faces blending and

sliding one in front of the other and the
voices are now the only mists around us

and they and our heartbeats are becoming
one as if really only our heartbeats are

what hear them not our ears

And our own voices begin to be
the sounds we hear now articulated from our

own throats and out our own mouths
reciting the very words of this poem

and seeing with the sounds we are
making what otherwise would be

invisible to our eyes and that
seeing is God seeing through us

and we are nowhere at all and seemingly
in a kind of everywhere being ourselves

repeated softly and warmly by the
extremely generous and continuous

descent through matter and out the
other side of it back into

space again where all is both
light and darkness and we are

simply specks again
afloat on God's breath

12/5

EXISTENCE AND EXTINCTION

Existence is time
heading towards

extinction

12/7

HERE AT THE CROSSROADS

Here at the crossroads of
Helplessness and Hope

the slightest sparrow's flight is
God's signature on my decree

and I'm always found wanting
in all the meanings of that word

Here trees shoot upward
clouds cross in their fleecy way

faces emerge and submerge again
without a wink

Helplessness is the way I got here and
where I stand

Hope is the little red Chihuahua
that follows along

known to the Aztecs as *Itzcuintli*

who leads them to the realm of death
faithful and already scorched

I too am squat-legged and bewildered
facing the beating sun

Shut off all outside
until the inside is alone

Time is our placid arbiter
until it's called out of the room

But each moment is inflated by
God's urgency to know Him in this

very moment's tight embrace

A bus will come and take me
away to the Land of the Forgotten

only the blind driver illumined by
inner sight knows how to find

but for now I'll wait here in
the beating sun

until true sunrise comes
and a blue moon

shows me the way home

12/13

I GO TO SLEEP

I go to sleep

like an illuminated feather

falling down

into blackness

12/15

METEOR SHOWER

I sit on the edge of my bed with a
chest of pearl and a brain of

sizzling silver

My feet have turned to wood
and my hands to squirrel hutches

There's an accompanying sizzle in the air
or in my ears it's hard to

tell

and outside it may snow onto the
sleeping alligators of the streets

There's a village celebration going on
way deep in the middle of my heart

though all the black horses have been
rounded up it's still pretty wild out there

and the general restlessness has grown
quiet in the harvest moonlight

Night never seems like night to me
and now that I'm nearing seventy

it seems less and less so

or is it day playing tricks on us with its
hustle and bustle keeping things in

tiptop shape as if both the
world and us would live forever?

I wonder who dusts the planets who
pours out the overflooded gulches who

wets the dry forests and keeps the
dogs from starving there on the

outermost orbits? But of course
only the Originator of them truly

maintains their distinctive personalities
and their survival in every conceivable

darkness and every illuminating
meteor shower however brief and

spectacular

12/18

ALL SIDES AT ONCE

In the case of the slobbering giant
the elves had no recourse but umbrellas

In the case of canoe over waterfall
the sailor could throw away his compass

In the case of ants who stole
grandma Atherton's cookies

the cookie crumb trail led to those
many tiny feet and happy mandibles

In the case of the unfathomable
mysteries of self and its endless

smokescreens subterfuges and disguises
where seductive graciousness and sparkling

personality have won everyone over
we have an almost uncrackable case

though the clues be left everywhere
while yet fresh fingerprints haven't even

left their fingers

In a high wind we react one way
in a calm we react another

We have our good days and our
bad but from one perspective

all days are God's radiance down a
kind of stairway of gradations that

nevertheless always reach us whether we're
ascending or descending

It's not a matter of chance but there are
some seeming arbitrary elements attached

while at the heart the nuggets of chrysoprase and
amber give out sensational attractors to inspire

earnest digging and intrepid pushing on

and a line of glorious arachnified
spiderweb that leads us not to the

all-devouring bull at the center but
to a divine noplace that lets light in from

all sides at once

12/21

CUL-DE-SAC

The cul-de-sac you find yourself in
the dead-end the *"dangerous curve ahead"*

doesn't resemble a flight of swans
or anything in this rotund creation that flows

forward or slides easily from one benign
landscape to another

The little windowless box that
was a room and now is a rodeo of

bodiless shouts and *huzzas* with no
palpable origin but plenty of hard body ghosts

The dead letters never sent falling
into your heart as if from a height

can't easily be changed it's true into something
light and easy just by saying so

or even you saying so to yourself though
the megaphone on the Hindenberg be in

your hands to alert the passengers to
jump to safety

The rope thrown down the well has been
grasped by your fist and needs only to be

pulled on to be pulled up and pulled out

The light on the lakes that illuminates the
swans just before takeoff was

created just for you and everyone
like you and

no one else but you

And when they do
take off their gorgeous white

flight in the sunlight is
also you make no mistake

against pellucid blue

12/23

IF THE ANGELS ARE HEARING

If the angels are hearing my
thoughts right now I'm doomed

And if they aren't
we're all doomed!

Find a corner where He can't
hear us or see us

Bring back your dead chicken
having said "He can't see me here"

or the unplugged loudspeaker of our
heart having said "He can't

hear me here"

with utter benignity
in a place where the roseate

hues of the universe are
modulating from dusk to dawn every

second of existence
and go from a fierce purple to

pale mauve or from blackest of black
to a spring hillside covered with

mustard flowers and fleecy sheep with their
placid faces

No smoky backroom too obscure
escapes His notice and

what goes on there
and the glance of the whale so

deep undersea none see it
but it is seen

in sweet serenity

I myself am held right now
in these parameters

toiling in the mindset
of freedom

but no more free than the
north side of a rock catching

the south side of sunlight
or the wild horse retaining its

wild horseness as it
leaps away

O angels hear us all
and take our plea!

12/25

WHEN WE SPEAK

When we speak a certain
pathetic beneficence

infuses our words

as if a slack clothesline were
strung from our tenement window to

others above a slovenly alleyway
and variously colored

garments some more intimate than
others were hung out to dry

The room fills with conversation the way
flamingos stand on a hill some with

heads tucked miraculously under wings
others unprecariously on one leg asleep

while some with their questioning stance
seem about to fly away

yet the room is empty and
only the softest of echoes reverberate

through it to the end that our
voices crash against a far wall slowly

like surf breaking into sizzle at the
finish of its intercontinental voyage

The heart is a stern
instructor on a hilltop and its

words are the coconut xylophone used
to transmit its music across the

tangled jungle to distant inhabited clearings

If I say *"I love you"* who am
I to say it and who are

you to hear it in the
cloud-flecked blue sky above us

and the deep ocean beneath us?

And when we go what
words will be left? What

schools of words will dart away?
What debris if any

remain? Then

"I love you" might fly back in the
window after a super-galactic flight

on tissue-thin paper signed by
its true origin in the

divine script of God's love
through which only that

endless blue sky can be seen

and in the far distance
the ever-turning world

12/26

LORD WEAR ME OUT

Lord wear me out in the saddle of Your
continuous gallop

over fences if You will or even
round and round in the same corral

if at each turn the light changes and
more and more beauty coheres and

shows its stunning body

You haven't led us here for stasis
with our urgent hearts inside doing all the

turning for us and containing both all the
lilies in their silver-white blooms

and the nights against whose gorgeous
blackness such lilies shine

Let me wander loose or tight-reigned
wild or tamed in Your perfect modulations

over transformative and transforming
landscapes as You desire them to be

seen
my own eyes blinded instead

by your Beauty alone

Peel me back Lord
Peel me way back to where only

You are here in the saddle
charging through the waterfall of the world

12/27

THE LONGEST MILE

The longest mile may be the
distance from our soul to the

apprehension of our soul

our mouth and where the
medicine must be taken to

do any good

our feet and putting them on the
ground to do compassionate

works that may be
nothing more than a glance at a

bird as it flies past

But I'm getting ahead of myself
a mile ahead of myself

I can't say I've been there or I'd be able to
call from a window and the

grass would water itself and the
trees step aside to let the

ghost herds of wingéd cattle through

And a single touch might awaken the
downtrodden to throw away the

anchor around their necks that are
sometimes clung to with such

ferocity

So that the longest mile is the
illusory distance between us and

the very person we are
but it sometimes has to pass through

countrysides of crazy to get there
and though no one's really there at the

beginning nor at the end
we must have the highest regard for that

no one to affect the long mile's shrinkage
and the embrace of light that

transforms us from ourselves

12/28

HE HAD THE TOUCH

He had the touch of miracles in his
hands and where his feet trod

turned to gold
I mean he'd step onto a cement

sidewalk but when we looked behind him
it had turned to gold

This may seem a fiction but aren't we
all a fiction as Wallace Stevens said

a *"Supreme Fiction"*?
What remains after we're gone but

more or less complex "literary"
memories in others

words in print or handwritten letters though
they may be totally ephemeral these days with

high technology erasing virtualities made now
even more fictive

And everything in creation coming from
The Word and going

back to it again in its purest
essence as pronounceable articulation spoken

God's enunciate metaphor this whole
universe in which we

move and breathe

holding axe handles and adzes
hammering or chipping away at

rock or wood to fashion a
habitable world that also

disappears but is kept alive in words

So his steps were golden and so were his
words golden words

Where he sat became sacred because
he was sacred and those who

sat with him became golden from his
golden touch and the turning-to-gold in

the hearts of those who heard him
that turned them to gold

if even for a moment

but malleable workable gold not
King Midas gold

miraculous sheen and burnish
which is how he left the

world behind him
and us

as he went

12/29

THE MAGNITUDE

The magnitude is impossible to deduce
from this side of the sky

From the other side of the sky
everything's possible

A man with a deer's head teaching mathematics to
a classroom of students who ring like bells

A plateau of goats on their hindlegs doing somersaults
as their shepherdess reads to them from tablets of silk

Astronomers who simply point to somewhere in the sky
and stars and planets call out their names

in audible voices as clear as trumpets

A land of waterfalls so plentifully lustrous
everyone's flotation devices are biologically supplied

A central globed arena rotating in ten different speeds of peacefulness
without seeming to move at all or ever come to anything like a stop

Migrating birds seen in one direction in profile
making the shape of our ecstatic faces sailing through blue sky

The staggeringly bright radiance that
floods God's universe

in dark shadow compared to the
workshop He works from

which is everywhere at once
and every time and every place

simultaneously present in the spark
suspended in air

which is this world we perceive and
grieve over so seriously

barely a blink of light
as it falls into our hands

leaving a star-shaped scar
that heals before it wounds

because the magnitude of all this is nearly
impossible to deduce

from anything anyone does or says
except the light in our eyes

and what our hearts recite
so precisely and gloriously

in the immeasurable magnitude
of a single heartbeat

1/2

INK

Spoke the angel *"You may
now take the ink from your bodies*

and drain it out drop by drop"

Our bodies just pens
writing

1/18

STARLIGHT

If you brush stars off your table
they'll scatter in the air like

orbiting crumbs

Whole giant fields of space surround them

Each one a kind of principality
unto itself

If you remain still such atomic anxieties
coalesce

Space snuggles in and a radiant center
makes its warm presence felt

We could travel through these spaces for a
thousand years and each inch forward would be

back at the beginning
such a perfect blue sky ahead

always receding

Don't you see
there are stars around your head

around your heart

Star shine dazzling your cheeks and eyes
in a splendor that simply

defies description

Shake some of the star spangles
out of your sleeves

Step out on starlight
impalpable starlight

No smoke there
no fuzzy demeanors

just starlight

1/23

THE THRONE PERPENDICULAR TO ALL THAT IS HORIZONTAL

1

The inebriate in the corner is the most
inebriated of them all

The moment he opens his eyes he
closes them again

They've draped a flag of no known
country across him

He stood up once turned 360° and
sat down again

I often wonder if he isn't dead
Then he opens his eyes and delivers a

spellbinding lecture for an hour
in which all tree boughs fill with

rainbow birds and the air is luminous

It seems when he does stand up he's
a doorway into elsewhere

But he slumps down again into the
corner and closes his eyes and

breathes the fumes of such drunkenness
anyone passing near him becomes

drunk as well

Bring out the forbidden stringed instrument and
play him a tune

It brings him to life

I seem to see a young man within him
spinning the stars

2

All he'll ever talk about is the
Throne perpendicular to all that is

horizontal

And he starts from where we are
saying that to the perpendicular Throne

everything's horizontally metaphorical

And to the God of the Throne even His
Throne's horizontally metaphorical

except He sits on it and the
universe is imbued with His Light

even to weeds and slow
cattle munching and chewing their cuds

as well as sun rays
falling on distant-most planets

and subtlest inhabitants of other
dimensions to this one

a place that is not a wilderness
but is a made place

each angle of it
each fiery restlessness

that eludes us no matter how
intimate we've become

when its knowledge dawns on us

God enters but can't be said to
enter that place perpendicular to

all else while yet there is
nothing inside nor outside the domain of His

horizontal as well as His
perpendicular Light

1/25

الله

INDEX

ABOUT THE AUTHOR

Born in 1940 in Oakland, California, Daniel Abdal-Hayy Moore had his first book of poems, *Dawn Visions*, published by Lawrence Ferlinghetti of City Lights Books, San Francisco, in 1964, and the second in 1972, *Burnt Heart/Ode to the War Dead*. He created and directed *The Floating Lotus Magic Opera Company* in Berkeley, California in the late 60s, and presented two major productions, *The Walls Are Running Blood*, and *Bliss Apocalypse*. He became a Sufi Muslim in 1970, performed the Hajj in 1972, and lived and traveled throughout Morocco, Spain, Algeria and Nigeria, landing in California and publishing *The Desert is the Only Way Out*, and *Chronicles of Akhira* in the early 80s (Zilzal Press). Residing in Philadelphia since 1990, in 1996 he published *The Ramadan Sonnets* (Jusoor/City Lights), and in 2002, *The Blind Beekeeper* (Jusoor/Syracuse University Press). He has been the major editor for a number of works, including *The Burdah* of Shaykh Busiri, translated by Hamza Yusuf, and the poetry of Palestinian poet, Mahmoud Darwish, translated by Munir Akash. He is also widely published on the worldwide web: *The American Muslim, DeenPort*, and his own website and poetry blog, among others: *www.danielmoorepoetry. com, www.ecstaticxchange.wordpress.com*. He has been poetry editor for *Seasons Journal, Islamica Magazine*, a 2010 translation by Munir Akash of *State of Siege*, by Mahmoud Darwish (Syracuse University Press), and *The Prayer of the Oppressed*, by Imam Muhammad Nasir al-Dar'i, translated by Hamza Yusuf. In 2011, 2012 and 2014 he was among the winners of the Nazim Hikmet Prize for Poetry. In 2013 he won an American Book Award for *Blood Songs*, and was listed among The 500 Most Influential Muslims for 2013 for his poetry. *The Ecstatic Exchange Series* is bringing out the extensive body of his works of poetry (a complete list of published works on page 2).

POETIC WORKS by Daniel Abdal-Hayy Moore
Published and Unpublished

Dawn Visions (published by City Lights, 1964)
Burnt Heart/Ode to the War Dead (published by City Lights, 1972)
This Body of Black Light Gone Through the Diamond (printed by Fred
    Stone, Cambridge, Mass, 1965)
On The Streets at Night Alone (1965?)
All Hail the Surgical Lamp (1967)
States of Amazement (1970)

Abdallah Jones and the Disappearing-Dust Caper (published by The
    Ecstatic Exchange/Crescent Series, 2006)
'Ala ud-Deen and the Magic Lamp (published by The Ecstatic Exchange, 2011)
The Chronicles of Akhira (1981) (published by Zilzal Press with
    Typoglyphs by Karl Kempton, 1986; published in Sparrow on the
    Prophet's Tomb by The Ecstatic Exchange, 2009)
Mouloud (1984) (A Zilzal Press chapbook, 1995; published in Sparrow on
    the Prophet's Tomb by The Ecstatic Exchange, 2009)
The Crown of Creation (1984) (published by The Ecstatic Exchange, 2012)
The Look of the Lion (The Parabolas of Sight) (1984)
The Desert is the Only Way Out (completed 4/21/84) (Zilzal Press chapbook,
    1985)
Atomic Dance (1984) (am here books, 1988)
Outlandish Tales (1984)
Awake as Never Before (12/26/84) (Zilzal Press chapbook, 1993)
Glorious Intervals (1/1/85) (Zilzal Press chapbook, ?)
Long Days on Earth/Book I (1/28 – 8/30/85)
Long Days on Earth/Book II (Hayy Ibn Yaqzan)
Long Days on Earth/Book III (1/22/86)
Long Days on Earth/Book IV (1986)
The Ramadan Sonnets (Long Days on Earth/Book V) (5/9 – 6/11/86)
    (published by Jusoor/City Lights Books, 1996) (republished as Ramadan
    Sonnets by The Ecstatic Exchange, 2005)
Long Days on Earth/Book VI (6-8/30/86)
Holograms (9/4/86 – 3/26/87)
History of the World (The Epic of Man's Survival) (4/7 – 6/18/87)
Exploratory Odes (6/25 – 10/18/87)

The Man at the End of the World (11/11 – 12/10/87)
The Perfect Orchestra (3/30 – 7/25/88)(published by The Ecstatic
    Exchange, 2009)
Fed from Underground Springs (7/30 – 11/23/88)
Ideas of the Heart (11/27/88 – 5/5/89)
New Poems (scattered poems, out of series, from 3/24 – 8/9/89)
Facing Mecca (5/16 – 11/11/89)
A Maddening Disregard for the Passage of Time (11/17/89 – 5/20/90)
    (published by The Ecstatic Exchange, 2009)
The Heart Falls in Love with Visions of Perfection (6/15/90 – 6/2/91)
Like When You Wave at a Train and the Train Hoots Back at You (Farid's
    Book) (6/11 – 7/26/91) (published by The Ecstatic Exchange, 2008)
Orpheus Meets Morpheus (8/1/91– 3/14/92)
The Puzzle (3/21/92 – 8/17/93)(published by The Ecstatic Exchange, 2011)
The Greater Vehicle (10/17/93 – 4/30/94)
A Hundred Little 3-D Pictures (5/14/94 – 9/11/95) (published by The Estatic
    Exchange, 2013)
The Angel Broadcast (9/29 – 12/17/95)
Mecca/Medina Time-Warp (12/19/95 – 1/6/96) (published as a Zilzal Press
    chapbook, 1996)(published in Sparrow on the Prophet's Tomb, 2009)
Miracle Songs for the Millennium (1/20 – 10/16/96)(published by The
    Ecstatic Exchange, 2014)
The Blind Beekeeper (11/15/96 – 5/30/97) (published 2002 by Jusoor/
    Syracuse University Press)
Chants for the Beauty Feast (6/3 – 10/28/97)(published by The Ecstatic
    Exchange, 2011)
You Open a Door and it's a Starry Night (10/29/97 – 5/23/98) (published by
    The Ecstatic Exchange, 2009)
Salt Prayers (5/29 – 10/24/98) (published by The Ecstatic Exchange, 2005)
Some (10/25/98 – 4/25/99)
Flight to Egypt (5/1 – 5/16/99)
I Imagine a Lion (5/21 – 11/15/99) (published by The Ecstatic Exchange,
    2006)
Millennial Prognostications (11/25/99 – 2/2/2000) (published by the Ecstatic
    Exchange, 2009)
Shaking the Quicksilver Pool (2/4 – 10/8/2000) (published by The Ecstatic
    Exchange, 2009)
Blood Songs (10/9/2000 – 4/3/2001)(Published by The Ecstatic Exchange,
    2012)

The Music Space (4/10 – 9/16/2001) (published by The Ecstatic Exchange, 2007)

Where Death Goes (9/20/2001 – 5/1/2002) (published by The Ecstatic Exchange, 2009)

The Flame of Transformation Turns to Light (99 Ghazals Written in English) (5/14 – 8/21/2002) (published by The Ecstatic Exchange, 2007)

Through Rose-Colored Glasses (7/22/2002 – 1/15/2003) (published by The Ecstatic Exchange, 2007)

Psalms for the Broken-Hearted (1/22 – 5/25/2003) (published by The Ecstatic Exchange, 2006)

Hoopoe's Argument (5/27 – 9/18/03)

Love is a Letter Burning in a High Wind (9/21 – 11/6/2003) (published by The Ecstatic Exchange, 2006)

Laughing Buddha/Weeping Sufi (11/7/2003 – 1/10/2004) (published by The Ecstatic Exchange, 2005)

Mars and Beyond (1/20 – 3/29/2004) (published by The Ecstatic Exchange, 2005)

Underwater Galaxies (4/5 – 7/21/2004) (published by The Ecstatic Exchange, 2007)

Cooked Oranges (7/23/2004 – 1/24/2005 (published by The Ecstatic Exchange, 2007)

Holiday from the Perfect Crime (1/25 – 6/11/2005)(published by The Ecstatic Exchange, 2011)

Stories Too Fiery to Sing Too Watery to Whisper (6/13 – 10/24/2005)

Coattails of the Saint (10/26/2005 – 5/10/2006) (published by The Ecstatic Exchange, 2006)

In the Realm of Neither (5/14/2006 – 11/12/06) (published by The Ecstatic Exchange, 2008)

Invention of the Wheel (11/13/06 – 6/10/07)(published by The Ecstatic Exchange, 2010)

The Sound of Geese Over the House (6/15 – 11/4/07)

The Fire Eater's Lunchbreak (11/11/07 – 5/19/2008) (published by The Ecstatic Exchange, 2008)

Sparks Off the Main Strike (5/24/2008 – 1/10/2009)(published by The Ecstatic Exchange, 2010)

Stretched Out on Amethysts (1/13 – 9/17/2009)(published by The Ecstatic Exchange, 2010)

The Throne Perpendicular to All that is Horizontal (9/18/09 – 1/25/10)(published by The Ecstatic Exchange, 2014)

In Constant Incandescence (2/10 – 8/13/10) (published by The Ecstatic
    Exchange, 2011)
The Caged Bear Spies the Angel (8/30/10 – 3/6/11)(published by The Ecstatic
    Exchange, 2010)
This Light Slants Upward (3/7 – 10/13/11)
Ramadan is Burnished Sunlight (part of This Light Slants Upward,
    published separately by The Ecstatic Exchange, 2011)
The Match That Becomes a Conflagration (10/14/11 – 5/9/12)
Down at the Deep End (5/10 – 8/3/12) (published by The Ecstatic
    Exchange, 2012)
Next Life (8/9/12 – 2/12/13) (published by The Ecstatic Exchange, 2013)
The Soul's Home (2/13 – 10/8/13)
Eternity Shimmers & Time Holds its Breath (10/10/13 – 1/27/14)
He Comes Running (part of Eternity Shimmers, published as an Ecstatic
    Exchange Chapbook, 2014)
The Sweet Enigma of it All (1/28/14 –)

www.ingramcontent.com/pod-product-compliance
Lightning Source LLC
Chambersburg PA
CBHW030712110426
R18122000003B/R181220PG42736CBX00011B/9